D0205460

Created by
Jordan Mechner

Written by
A. B. Sina

Artwork by
LeUyen Pham & Alex Puvilland

Color by
Hilary Sycamore

PRINCE of PERSIA

THE GRAPHIC NOVEL

:01

First Second
New York & London

THE FOLLOWING LEGENDS OF PRINCES AND PROPHETS, GARDENS AND GRAVES, WATER AND FIRE, WILL NOT BE FOUND IN BOOKS OF HISTORY. ANY RESEMBLANCES TO REAL PEOPLE, PLACES, OR EVENTS MAY BE BLAMED ON THE VIVID IMAGINATION OF THE READER.

HOW CAN YOU TELL...

...WHEN YOUR TIME HAS COME?

KILL HIM AND YOU'LL HAVE A REBELLION ON YOUR HANDS. OUR PEOPLE WON'T STAND FOR IT.

YOUR PEOPLE?

YOUR PEOPLE ARE OUT THERE...

MARV, 9TH CENTURY A.D.

AND YOU'RE HERE, IN A PALACE. DO YOU THINK THEY CARE ABOUT THE ROSE PETALS IN YOUR POOL?

LAYTH, HE'S OUR BROTHER.

HE'S YOUR BROTHER. NOT MINE. NOT ANYMORE.

I'M FORGETTING...

I'M ALONE.

FORGIVE HIM OR YOU WILL NOT SEE ME ALIVE AGAIN...

I WANT TO DO THE OTHER DANCE.

YOUR FATHER PAYS ME TO TEACH YOU THIS ONE.

MARV, 13ᵗʰ CENTURY A.D.

BUT I DON'T HAVE THE HIPS, ARSALAN, YOU SAID IT YOURSELF...

I'M MADE FOR BACKFLIPS!!

SHIRIN, IF HE EVER FINDS OUT...

I SWEAR I HAVEN'T TOLD, NEVER WILL! A SECRET DANCE IS A SECRET DANCE.

COME ON, ARSALAN, LET'S WHIRL!

THE IDEAL ...

... OF THE FORMLESS.

ZBAM!!

THIS IS OUR LAST LESSON.

SORRY?

YOUR FATHER'S ORDERS. I AM NOT TO RETURN.

MY FATHER! THAT...! BUT WHY!?

NOT SURE, BUT IT'S PROBABLY WORSE NEWS FOR ME THAN YOU.

THERE ARE THINGS IN THE CITY YOU DON'T KNOW ABOUT, SHIRIN...

13

MOM, DAD, OTHER FOOLS, I WILL NEVER DANCE FOR YOU AGAIN.

OUTTA HERE, BEGGAR BOY!!

TAKE THE RAISINS, IT'S ALL WE HAVE, BUT THEY'RE GREENER THAN EMERALDS.

YOU SHOULD BE ASHAMED, ROBBING US LIKE BASTARD CHILDREN.

REMEMBER, GRANDPA, WE'RE HERE TO PROTECT YOU.

I'M TOO EARLY.

HEY SKINNY, WHY DON'T YOU HELP WITH THE WATER INSTEAD OF LOAFING AROUND LIKE A POET?

ME?? EEH YES OF COURSE...

YOUR MAMA STUFFED YOU WITH COTTON BALLS, SKINNY?

MY NAME ISN'T SKINNY! IT'S SH.... SHAPUR!

STOP THE FOOLING, BOYS. WHAT'S THE TROUBLE?

SKINNY HERE CAN'T PULL HIS BUCKET.

I SAID, MY NAME'S SHAPUR!!

STUCK, THANKS TO SKINNY.

SHAPUR MY NAME IS SH....

KLAK!!

YOUR NAME IS DONKEY TURD! NOW GET DOWN THERE AND FIX IT!

THE GREAT GHOST IS COMING TO GET YOOOOO !!!

FSHHH

HE SAID THE TREE WITH THE SIGN NEAR THE OLD WELL.

WHERE IS HE?

SWEAR THIS, SWEAR THAT,

THIS IS A SECRET, THAT'S A SECRET, THE BASTARD BETTER SHOW UP!

TRAITOR! LIAR! ARSALAN, YOU'RE NO LION! YOU'RE A DOG!

NO WAY I'M GOING BACK HOME. MAYBE I COULD JOIN THE NEXT CARAVAN TO BAGHDAD, IF I SELL MY PENDANT...

YOU'RE NOT ARSALAN.

AAH, MY HEAD HURTS...

GUIV, YOU CAN'T LEAVE.

LAYTH'S FORGIVEN YOU. THE PALACE BELONGS TO US, GUIV. AND WE BELONG TO IT.

YOU BELONG, LAYTH BELONGS, ME? FORGET ME. REMEMBER THE GUIV YOU KNEW.

YOU'RE TALKING NONSENSE.

NEAR DEATH, I SAW THINGS BEYOND WORDS.

YOU HAVE NOWHERE TO GO!

SHHHHOOO, GO BACK TO THE PALACE. GO!

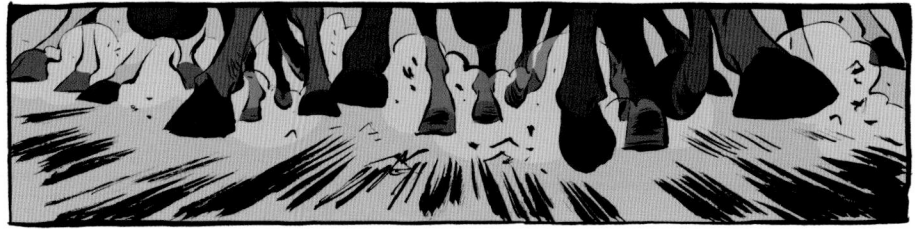

WE ARE PREPARED, PRINCE, TO BATTLE ALONGSIDE YOU TO THE END.

DO YOU EVEN KNOW THE END?

WHAT WE MEAN TO SAY, PRINCE, IS IT'S OUR DUTY TO FIGHT AND DIE FOR YOU.

YOUR DUTY, THEN, IS TO FIGHT AND DIE FOR NOBODY.

YOU WASTE YOUR TIME, YAAHR. NO INVISIBLE PROPHET THERE.

HOW DO YOU KNOW? EVERYONE SAYS THAT'S WHERE HE IS.

YOU HUNT UP HERE, WITH YOUR LAYTH AND YOUR SISTER, YES?

I USED TO.

THEN YOU KNOW NO ONE LIVES IN CITADEL.

YOU HEARD ME OR NO? NO ONE'S UP THERE, YAAAHR. AND STILL YOU ARE CLIMBING.

I NEED TO GET THERE.

YOU NEED WINGS, YAAHR.

ALL I NEED ARE LEGS.

TRICK IS TO GET ON TOP, LIKE A HORSE. THE CLAWS CAN'T BEND BACKWARDS...

...AND THEN THUMP.

I'VE SEEN YOU BEFORE.

NO ONE GAVE ME THE POWER TO TAKE LIFE.

NO ONE GAVE YOU POWER TO <u>SPARE</u> LIFE, YAAAHR.

WHAT ARE YOU, A PHILOSOPHER BIRD?

JUST AN OLD BIRD. IN A THOUSAND YEARS YOU ARE WISE TOO.

NO REST? WHAT? NOT THIRSTY? HUNGRY?

LEAVE ME ALONE, PEACOCK!

SEE YOU UP THERE, MAYBE.

CLAK

YAAAHR, LEGS NOT ENOUGH.

YAAAHRR!

EXACTLY WHAT I SAW WHEN I WAS DROWNING. I SAW THE CITADEL FROM UP HERE.

AND I SAW MYSELF BUT I WASN'T ME. I WAS ALREADY THIS OTHER ME IN THE CITADEL. UNDERSTAND?

YAAHR, I LIVE A THOUSAND YEARS.

GUILAN!

WHO'S GUILAN?
WHERE AM I?

I'M GLAD TO SEE YOU'RE FEELING BETTER, GUILAN.

MY NAME ISN'T GUILAN, IT'S SHAPUR.

BUT THAT'S A BOY'S NAME.

I AM A BOY.

NOT WHEN YOUR CLOTHES ARE WET.

OK. MY NAME'S SHIRIN, WHO ARE YOU?

THE SUN'S GOING, QUICK, TO THE PALACE.

PALACE? WHAT PALACE?

THIS IS A GARDEN AND FANCY IS ITS GARDENER. THE TREES CAN HEAR US.

IF THEY LIKE THE STORIES... THEY GIVE BACK FRUIT.

YOU'RE A VERY STRANGE PERSON.

WHY DID YOU CALL ME GUILAN?

LOOK! THE PRINCE.

WHAT? I DON'T SEE ANYONE.

UNLEARN YOUR EYES.

DON'T REMOVE THEM UNTIL YOU HEAR THE PRINCE'S FOOTSTEPS...

WHO ARE YOU?

I AM LAYTH, RULER OF MARV, PRINCE OF RUINS. AND YOU ARE PRINCESS GUILAN. YOUR BROTHER GUIV WAS HEIR TO THIS THRONE.

MY WHAT? MY...

OH, I GET IT... YES, MY BROTHER...

HE TRIED TO KILL ME.

YOU STOLE MY BROTHER'S THRONE! I HATE YOU!

NO, NO, YOU ARE MY PRINCESS. YOU ARE GUILAN.

ME GUILAN? YOU LAYTH?

THERE ARE TWO KINDS OF WARRIORS: THOSE WHO DESTROY AND LOOT AND THOSE WHO DESTROY AND REBUILD.

YOUR FATHER, SAMAN, SACKED THE CITY AND DEFEATED THE CALIPH'S ARMY.

THAT MAN, WITH HIS HEAD HANGING BY THE SKIN, IS THE CALIPH'S COMMANDER, MAMUN. MY FATHER, KILLED BY YOUR FATHER.

SAMAN REBUILT THE CITY TO GREATER SPLENDOR STILL... WITH CARAVAN SERAIS, BAZAARS, A LIBRARY...

AND A WATERWAY SYSTEM, CHANNELING WATER FROM THE MOUNTAINS AND THE RIVER TO THE CITY...

WATER FOR ALL.

AND AS FOR ME, LAYTH—HIS ENEMY'S SON—SAMAN RAISED ME AS HIS OWN.

WAIT...

... YOU DREW ALL THESE?

... YES ... AND EVERY CORNER HAS A STORY ...

... AND EVERY STORY A PRINCE, AND EVERY PRINCE, A PRINCESS, AND EVERY PRINCESS, A PEACOCK, AND EVERY PEACOCK A...

OK, OK, WAIT, SO IF SAMAN KILLED YOUR FATHER, THIS WAS YOUR THRONE

IT IS HIS THRONE WHO SITS ON IT.

GUIV, GUILAN, LAYTH –

IN THE "HOUSE OF STRENGTH," WE WERE EQUALS.

GUIV!

WHY ARE THREE CHILDREN BEFORE ME WHEN I CALLED ONLY ONE NAME?

FOR I AM THE PRINCE.

CHILDREN CAN DRIVE A KING TO MADNESS.

SO YOU SEE, GUILAN... YOU HAD A TWIN BROTHER, BUT TRULY IT IS YOU AND I WHO ARE INSEPARABLE.

LOOK, THIS IS FUN... BUT SERIOUSLY ... I NEED TO GET HOME.

YOU ARE HOME. YOU ARE GUILAN. THIS IS YOUR PALACE.

NO, I'M SHIRIN... AND YOU... I DON'T KNOW WHO YOU ARE... SOME WEIRD GUY WHO LIVES IN THE RUINS!

I'M FERDOS... GUARDIAN OF THE WATERS.

AT LEAST EAT SOMETHING BEFORE YOU GO.

THAT'S THE FIRST SENSIBLE THING YOU'VE SAID ALL NIGHT.

ALL THAT KOHL! WHAT DO YOU DO WITH ALL THAT KOHL?

IT'S GOOD FOR DRAWING.

HEY, DON'T WASTE THAT...

THE LION TAUGHT ME A DANCE...

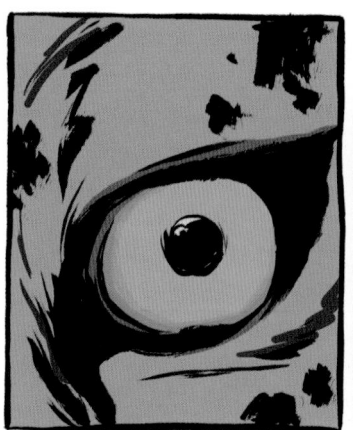

WILL HEAL FAST, YAAHR.

I GOT LUNCH.

I FEEL LIKE FIGS.

WHAT'S THIS?

TURNIP, YAAHR.

I SAID FIG, NOT TURNIP.

SO I HAVE TURNIP, NOT FIG. YOU WANT OR NO?

THIS PLACE IS GOING TO BE COLD.

YOU LOOK OUTSIDE, THE FIRE'S INSIDE, YAAHR.

WHY OPEN?

BECAUSE, PEACOCK, THAT'S WHAT A DOOR IS FOR.

YAAAAHR.

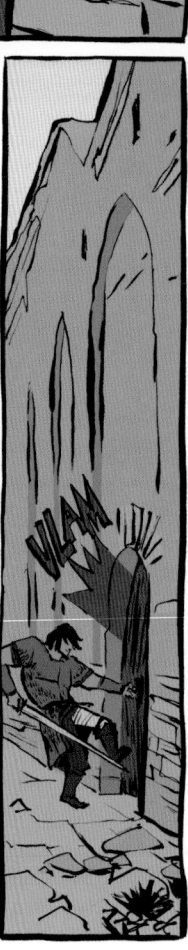

A DOOR IS ALSO FOR TO BE CLOSED, YAAHR.

TURUL ... WHAT ARE ALL THESE SKELETONS DOING HERE?

NOTHING. DEAD DO NOTHING, YOU KNOW?

TURUL!

THIS IS TOWER OF SILENCE.

THE OLD PRIESTS, THEY LAY OUT THE DEADS FOR VULTURES TO EAT. AND VULTURES, THEY EAT.

UNTIL THE END, WHEN DEAD ARE ONLY BONES.

THOUSAND THOUSAND YEARS, YAAHR.

THE EYE, IT SEES ME!

SO IT'S AN EYE, YAAHR.

PLEASE SEARCH...

...EVERY CORNER, CRACK, CRANNY... THE PEACOCK MUST BE SOMEWHERE!

SALE OF SILK AND PAPER FROM STATE MILLS, SUBLIME RULER OF MARV...

APPROVED.

TITHES ON CARAVANS AND LAND, SUBLIME RULER...

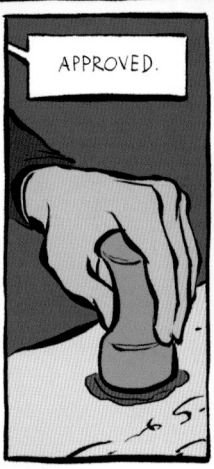

APPROVED.

THE WELLS HAVE WATER, SUBLIME RULER, THE CANALS ARE IN GOOD CONDITION.

ALL WATER NEEDS ARE BEING MET.

APP...

MY SOLDIERS NEED MORE WATER.

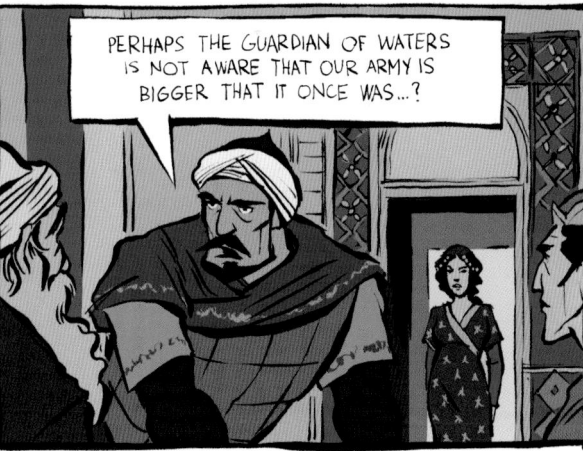

PERHAPS THE GUARDIAN OF WATERS IS NOT AWARE THAT OUR ARMY IS BIGGER THAT IT ONCE WAS...?

PRINCESS GUILAN. THE LIGHT FOLLOWS YOU, ILLUMINATING OUR PATHS.

I'M SURE YOU COULD FIND YOUR WAY JUST AS WELL IN DARKNESS, GENERAL.

AND YOUR ARMY IS BIG ENOUGH AS IT IS.

NOT APPROVED.

YOUR HIGHNESS, OUR CITIES MUST BE PROTECTED FROM ATTACK.

ATTACK FROM WHOM, GENERAL?

FROM THE PRINCESS'S BROTHER, FOR ONE.

WE HAVE NO CAUSE TO FEAR GUIV.

DO NOT FORGET, LAYTH, HOW YOU CAME TO THIS THRONE. A WEAK PRINCE IS NOT THE CALIPH'S IDEAL CHOICE.

GNNN...

I KNOW THE PHYSICIAN SAID YOU MUST EAT FIGS, MY LIGHT. BUT YOU MUSTN'T DROP THE SKINS EVERYWHERE.

AHHHHH! NOTHING WORKS!

I LOVE THAT SMELL, THE FIRST DROPS OF RAIN ON DRY DUST.

LIE WITH ME.

TELL ME— WOULD YOU REALLY HAVE DONE IT? WOULD YOU HAVE KILLED YOURSELF AND OUR CHILD?

MY LIGHT, WE GO THROUGH THIS EVERY DAY. STOP TORMENTING YOURSELF. WE CAN'T LIVE IN THE PAST.

IN THIS PALACE...

...EVERY CRACK IN A TILE...

...EVERY PATCH OF SHADE...

...EVERY STITCH IN A QUILT...

...THROWS ME AN IMAGE.

THERE IS ONLY THE PAST.

OUR CHILD IS NOT THE PAST, MY LIGHT.

HOW CAN YOU SEE WHERE YOU ARE GOING?

I DON'T NEED TO SEE.

I KNOW ALL THE WELLS AND TUNNELS.

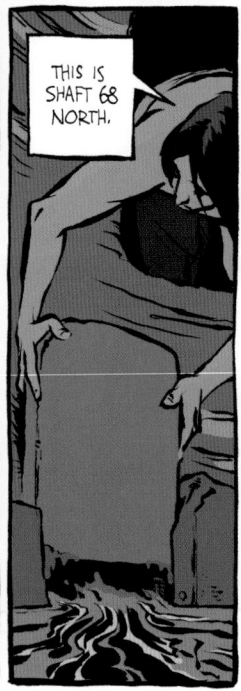

THIS IS SHAFT 68 NORTH.

IT TAKES THE WATER WHERE IT NEEDS TO GO.

THAT'S ENOUGH FOR NOW.

THESE WELLS ARE OLD— OLD FROM THE TIME OF LAYTH AND GUILAN. NO ONE KNOWS THEY EXIST ANYMORE.

CATCH!

MY TIME HAS COME, YOU ARE THREE, BUT THE THRONE HAS BUT ONE SEAT.

GUIV AS MY HEIR WILL CARRY MY NAME INTO THE FUTURE.

... WHILE TAKING CONTROL, NOT A DROP OF BLOOD, OF COURSE, THIS IS NOT FOR MY GAIN. I, AMIR, AM ONLY THE OBEDIENT SERVANT OF THE CALIPH IN BAGHDAD,

ON BEHALF OF WHOM I OFFER THE CITY OF MARV TO LAYTH.

I SHAN'T ACCEPT.

AS YOU CAN SEE, WE HAVE BEEN DELICATE...

IF YOU ACCEPT, PEACE WILL FOLLOW, YOUR FRIENDS WILL NOT BE HARMED; THEY'LL CONTINUE TO ENJOY THE PRIVILEGES OF NOBILITY: HUNTING, FEASTING, PLAYING...

FIFTY THOUSAND? YOU CAN WAGE WAR AND DESTROY MARV... OR YOU CAN LET LAYTH GOVERN.

IF YOU REFUSE, THERE WILL BE BLOODSHED.

WE'LL FIGHT TO THE END.

HOW MUCH IS YOUR PRIDE WORTH, GUIV? HOW MANY DEATHS? A THOUSAND?

AFTER ALL, ARE YOU THREE NOT ALL EQUALS?

LEGEND SAYS LAYTH WAS A GREAT RULER AND A SAD MAN. I THINK I WAS A SAD RULER AND A GREAT MAN.

AND ME?

...AND YOU...

AND YOU, EVERY TIME YOU LOOKED UPON ME, I SHONE BRIGHTER THAN THE MOON.

NO, I MEAN WHAT DOES THE LEGEND SAY ABOUT ME?

EVER SINCE YOU PUT ON GUILAN'S ROBES I CAN'T TELL ANYMORE.

WELL, I THINK, I THINK...

... I WANT TO DANCE NOW.

DANCE? I...I DON'T KNOW HOW TO, I NEVER REALLY...

I'LL TEACH YOU, AS THE LION TAUGHT ME...

IN THIS DANCE THE MOST IMPORTANT THING IS TO FORGET... YOUR BODY... MIND... FORM...

HEY! I WASN'T FINISHED DANCING...

THEY MUSTN'T SEE US!

WHY ARE WE HIDING?

NO ONE KNOWS I'M HERE. IF THEY FIND ME, THEY'LL KILL ME.

WHAT! WHY?

FLIP FLOP FLIP

LISTEN: CAMEL HOOFS FLIP-FLOPPING AWAY.

ONE SECOND YOU'RE A PRINCE ...THE NEXT YOU'RE HIDING LIKE A THIEF... AND NOW YOU'RE SNORTING AROUND IN THE DIRT LIKE A PIG. EXPLAIN YOURSELF!

THEY ALWAYS DROP SOMETHING.

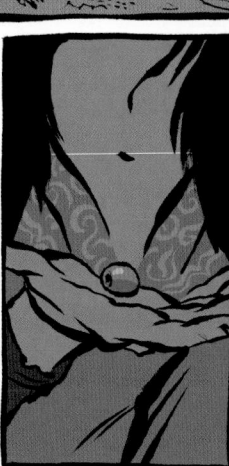

THAT'S IT, I WANT THAT CHANNEL COMPLETELY BLOCKED.

YOU'RE NO GUARDIAN OF THE WATERS, YOU'RE A WATER THIEF! WE HAVE NOTHING TO EAT!

GUARDS! LET THEM BE.

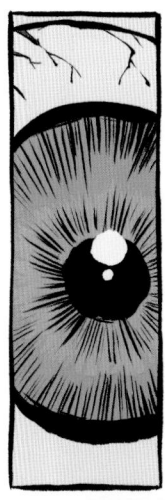

THEY SAY GUIV IS PREPARING HIS REVENGE ... HE WILL COME DOWN FROM THE HILLS WITH AN ARMY ...

WHAT A MISFORTUNE THAT WOULD BE. LAYTH HAS BEEN GOOD.

LAYTH - BAH! HE'S NOT EVEN FROM HERE.

I GOT THIS RING FROM A JEW, THIS FROM A BUDDHIST, THIS FROM A TURK. WHICH ONE DOESN'T BELONG?

DO NOT BELIEVE THOSE WHO SPREAD RUMORS TO CREATE FEAR ...

I HOPE GUIV STAYS IN WHATEVER HOLE HE'S HIDING IN.

THERE WILL BE NO ATTACK. WE ARE IN NO DANGER.

NO ONE CAN TELL WHAT WILL HAPPEN.

IF ONLY THE INVISIBLE PROPHET OF MARV RETURNED, HE COULD TELL US.

LIGHT OF THE CITY, IT IS NOT SAFE FOR YOU TO RIDE WITHOUT GUARDS.

LET ME PROTECT YOU.

THOUSAND THOUSAND...

THOUSAND THOUSAND...

THOUSAND THOUSAND...

THOUSAND THOUSAND YEARS

HAAHAHAHAAHA

HUF

HUF

HUF

HUF

THEY'RE **CHILDREN**... BABIES!

AAAAHHHHH...

MAY YOUR SHADOWS GROW LONG OVER US!

YOU ARE THE CROWN THAT SITS ON OUR HEADS.

MAY WE BE YOUR SACRIFICE!

WE ARE YOUR SERVANTS.

WHAT DOES GENERAL AMIR WANT FROM YOU?

I LIKE TO THINK HE WANTS ME TO SLIT HIS THROAT.

THAT WOULD SOLVE NOTHING, MY LIGHT. ONE MAN'S BLOOD LEADS TO ANOTHER'S.

LIGHT OF MY EYE, I WISH IT WERE GUIV ON THE THRONE AND ME OUTSIDE SOMEWHERE IN THE MOUNTAINS... FREE... WITH YOU.

IT'S FUNNY. EVERYONE IN THE WORLD IS DYING TO GET INTO THAT PALACE...

... AND YOU WANT TO GET OUT.

WHY ALL THESE QUESTIONS? AREN'T YOU HAPPY HERE?

YES... BUT... I DON'T KNOW ANYTHING ABOUT YOU.

THEN LET'S KEEP IT THAT WAY. YOU DON'T HAVE A PAST. I DON'T HAVE A PAST...

THAT'S WHY WE'RE HAPPY - BECAUSE IT'S JUST YOU AND ME.

OK, BUT COME ON — YOU LIVE IN A RUIN!

AND YOU'VE NEVER BEEN TO THE CITY? NOT EVEN ONCE? NEVER? NOT EVEN TO BUY BREAD?

BAD THINGS HAPPEN OUT THERE.

AND HERE? DON'T BAD THINGS HAPPEN HERE?

HERE...

THE STARS COME DOWN AND TEACH HISTORY A LESSON.

THE STARS ARE UP THERE. YOU CAN'T BRING THEM DOWN HERE.

I CAN, I WILL BRING THE STARS DOWN FOR YOU... LIGHT OF MY EYES...

LET'S TEACH THE STARS WHAT IT'S LIKE TO BE A FULL MOON.

IS THIS PART OF THE STORY?

I THINK THE GARDEN LIKES OUR STORY.

IT LIKES WATER TOO.

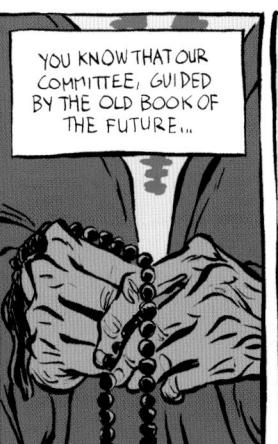
YOU KNOW THAT OUR COMMITTEE, GUIDED BY THE OLD BOOK OF THE FUTURE...

...BY THE VEILED PROPHET OF MARV, HAS FREQUENTLY IDENTIFIED SIGNS OF DANGER AND CRISIS...

...AND INSTITUTED MEASURES TO PROTECT US AND OUR CITY.

AS YOU WILL SURELY RECALL, GUARDIAN.

YES, SIR.

AS GUARDIAN OF THE WATER, IT IS YOUR RESPONSIBILITY TO SEE THAT ALL WATER REACHES THE PRINCE'S ROYAL ORCHARDS.

WATER...

YOU MAY GO.

LOTS OF WATER.

I WOULD GET RID OF HIM.

IT'S NOT THAT EASY. THE WELLS ARE AN OLD, COMPLEX HYDRAULIC SYSTEM. THEIR GUARDIANSHIP HAS BEEN IN THAT FAMILY FOR CENTURIES. NO ONE ELSE HAS THE EXPERTISE.

PUT A TAIL ON HIM. ALSO, INCREASE SECURITY ALL AROUND.

SECURITY, SECURITY,

I'LL SEE TO IT THAT ALL SUSPICIOUS PERSONS ARE IMMEDIATELY ARRESTED.

HOW DO WE KNOW WHO IS SUSPICIOUS?

IF THEY RESIST ARREST, THEY ARE SUSPICIOUS.

SECURITY, SECURITY, SECURITY...

SECURITY, SECURITY, SECURITY...

SECURITY, SECURITY...

GOVERNOR, I'VE BEEN MEANING TO MENTION— THE GUARDS COULD REALLY USE NEW UNIFORMS. THEIRS ARE QUITE OUT OF STYLE.

HAHA! WE SHOULD CHANGE YOUR TITLE TO GUARDIAN OF GOOD TASTE. BY THE WAY, ALI, WHEN IS YOUR NEXT PARTY?

EVERY NIGHT, GOVERNOR. EVERY NIGHT, YOU MUST JOIN US AGAIN SOON.

BETTER YET—WHY DON'T YOU HAVE ONE HERE AT THE PALACE? THE PRINCE LIKES PARTIES, DON'T YOU, UNCLE?

PARTY, PARTY, PARTY...

OUF...

THIS USED TO BE EASIER. I'M GETTING OLD.

BASTARDS THINK THEY CAN KEEP A WATCH ON ME.

FERDOS.

YES, YES, I'M HERE.

FRESH BREAD.

THANK YOU.

COME WITH ME.

YOU LEFT IT OPEN ALL NIGHT! IDIOT — WHAT WERE YOU THINKING?

I... FELL ASLEEP.

YOU GAVE THEM SO MUCH WATER, IT WAS NOTICED.

WE HAVE TO STOP FOR NOW, UNDERSTOOD?

FERDOS?

?

SQUEEK
SQUEEK

SQUEEK
SQUEEK
SQUEEK

WE MIGHT
NEED THESE.

THERE ARE THINGS
IN THE CITY YOU
DON'T KNOW ABOUT

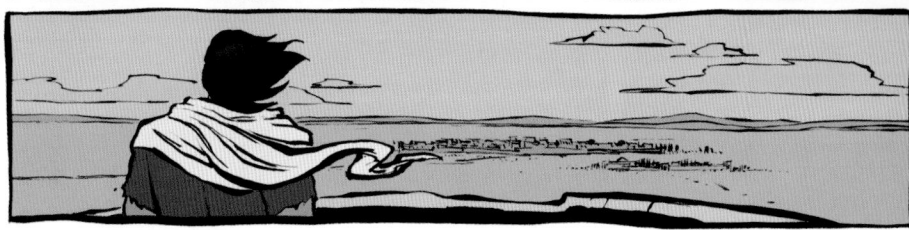

GUEEEE, WHHAAA YYYYOOOGGGEE...

SOWWY, MY TONGUE 'TH ATHLEEP. YAAAAAHHRR.

I ASKED, WHERE YOU ARE GOING.

UP THE STAIRS.

AND THEN DOWN. TWENTY-EIGHT TIMES A DAY, EVERY DAY, SIX MONTHS. YAAHR. BUT WHERE YOU ARE GOING?

WHERE DOES ANYONE GO, PEACOCK? AT LEAST WHEN I GO UP IT FEELS GOOD TO GO UP...

... AND WHEN I COME DOWN IT FEELS GOOD TO COME DOWN,

ALWAYS YOU NEED SOMETHING TO LOOK FORWARD TO?

AND YOU? ALWAYS YOU NEED TO CACKLE CACKLE?

WHAT AM I DOING HERE? MY TWIN, MY BLOOD, MY PAST ARE FAR AWAY. I DO FEEL ANOTHER FUTURE COMING... BUT HOW LONG MUST I WAIT?

YOU DON'T KNOW FROM WAITING, YAAHR. IN THREE HUNDRED YEARS HOW MANY TIMES YOU WILL UP-AND-DOWN THE STAIRS?

KRAK

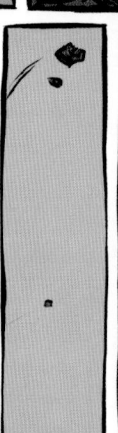

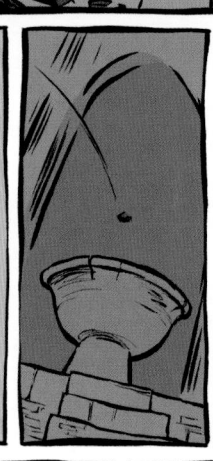

WHAT IS THIS?

I TELL YOU FIRST DAY: FIRE IS INSIDE. AND YOU SAY I JUST CACKLE.

TOWER OF FIRE. FOR LIGHT. FOR TO SEE.

TURUL, I SEE THINGS...

... FIRES, BONES, RUINS, THE END OF EVERYTHING.

THERE ARE MANY ENDS BEFORE THE END, YAHHHR. WHAT YOU SEE IS LITTLE SOMETHINGS OF FUTURE.

WHOSE FUTURE?

TURUL? WHERE ARE YOU GOING?

FIRE IS HAZARD. YAAHR. TOO MANY FEATHERS.

WAIT, TURUL!

YAAAHR!

TURUL! DON'T LEAVE ME HERE!

EGGS, QUAIL EGGS, CHICKEN EGGS, PIGEON EGGS...

WHAT DO THE LEAVES SAY ABOUT MY FUTURE, HAKIM?

MY DEAR HUSSEIN, YOUR FUTURE IS EMPTY.

HOW CAN YOU EXPECT ME TO READ YOUR TEA LEAVES WHEN YOU'VE SWALLOWED THEM ALL?

HAHAHA!

BAM
BAM
BAM

WHO...? TURUL?
NO, NO, BIRDS
DON'T KNOCK
...SO?

NO...

NO ONE KNOWS
THAT GUIV IS HERE.

AND IN FACT HE'S NOT.

I SAW YOUR FLAME LAST NIGHT AS I SAT IN EGG GOO, BLESSED ONE. I WALKED ALL NIGHT AND AM HAPPY ONLY TO STAY BEHIND YOUR CLOSED DOOR.

WE HAVE WAITED SO LONG...

... AND NOW I KNEEL HERE BEFORE YOU WITH TWO QUESTIONS:

WILL MY SON'S WIFE FINALLY GIVE US THE DOWRY? AND WILL MY BUNION STOP HURTING?

THANK YOU, VEILED ONE. THANK YOU FOR LETTING ME ASK!

THE VEILED ONE IS THERE, I SAW HIM!

WHAT DID HE LOOK LIKE?

HIS FACE WAS COVERED!

OF COURSE! FOR EVEN HAD HE APPEARED, WE MAY NOT SEE HIM!

AND WHAT DID HE SAY?

NOTHING!

YES! FOR EVEN HAD HE SPOKEN, WE MAY NOT HEAR HIM!

IT WAS ENOUGH FOR ME JUST TO LAY EYES ON THE VEILED PROPHET OF MARV.

SO?

SHHH! I CAN HEAR HIM PRAYING.

TURUL! WHAT DO I DO?

TURUL?

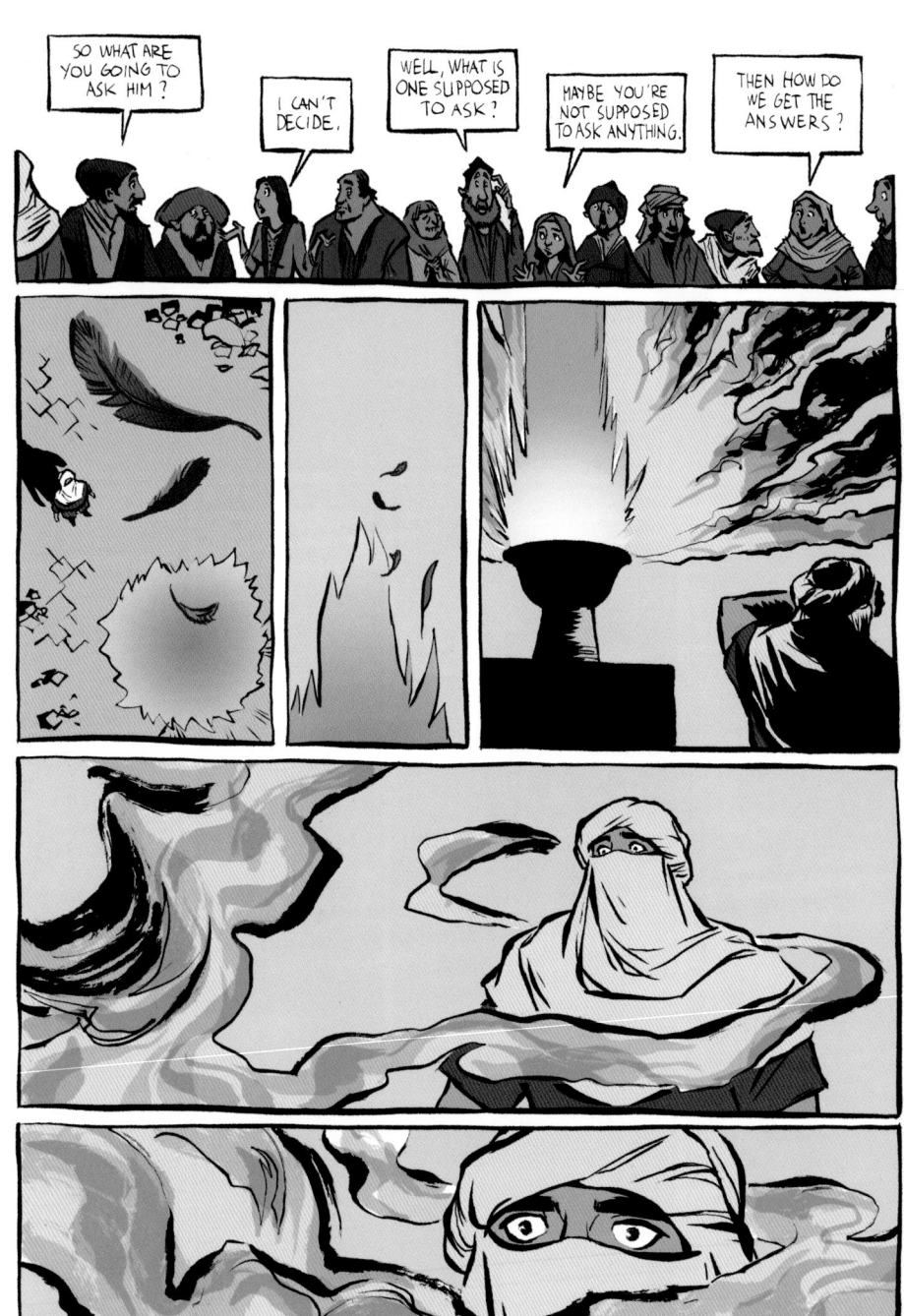

WE MUST REMEMBER THE FUTURE ...

... FOR THE FUTURE REMEMBERS US.

A MAN MUST BE BORN FROM A WOMB LIKE ANY OTHER WOMB, UNDER THE THIRD FULL MOON...

... FROM HENCE TWO HUNDRED AND FORTY-ONE YEARS OF THE MOON, THE KILLER OF ALL RULERS AND ALL THE RULED...

A PALACE MUST FALL ...

A PRINCE MUST RISE FROM THE WATERS WHERE NONE HAS KNOWN HIM...

... SAVE FOR A SAD GIRL UNDER A FIG TREE...

I CURSE THE CALENDAR, I CURSE TIME FOR ITS INSOLENCE ...

IN THE TIME OF OUR ANCESTORS, A PROPHECY WAS MADE.

ON THE THIRD FULL MOON, IN THE 481ST YEAR OF THE MOON ...

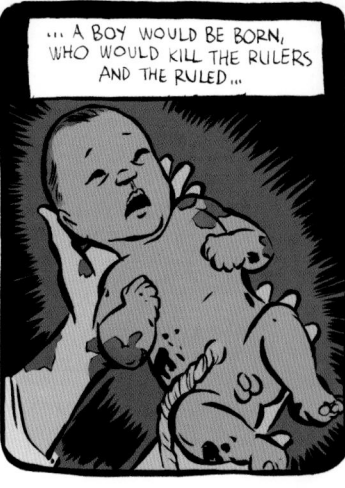

... A BOY WOULD BE BORN, WHO WOULD KILL THE RULERS AND THE RULED ...

AS THE PROPHESIED DAY APPROACHED, OUR RULERS FORMED THE COMMITTEE.

OUR ENEMY IS AMONGST US. EXTRAORDINARY MEASURES ARE NECESSARY ...

A RECORD OF ALL PREGNANT WOMEN SHALL BE KEPT.

ALL BOYS BORN ON THE PROPHESIED DAY SHALL BE CONFISCATED BY THE STATE.

ON THE EVE OF THE FULL MOON, EVERY PREGNANT WOMAN IN MARV PRAYED.

CHILD, IF YOU ARE A SON, DELAY YOUR ARRIVAL INTO THIS WORLD.

ALL EXCEPT ONE...

YOU, WHO CANNOT SPEAK... FORGIVE ME.

YOU WILL FORGET AND HEAL AND HAVE ANOTHER ONE.

WAAAAA AAAAA!

DO NOT FEAR, HE WILL BE IN STATE CUSTODY.

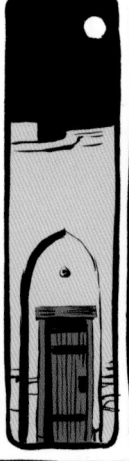

A BOY.

MOTHER, ARE YOU READY TO ...

AAAAHHH ...

SHE DIED IN CHILDBIRTH.

WHAT ABOUT THE CHILD? BOY OR GIRL?

STILLBORN, MOTHER AND CHILD, BOTH DEAD.

THERE IS AN OLD LEGEND IN OUR HOUSE: THREE HUNDRED YEARS AGO, MY ANCESTORS SAVED A PRINCESS BY HIDING HER IN A WELL.

WHEN THEY BUILT THE NEW WELLS, MY GRANDFATHER DUG A SECRET TUNNEL...

... CONNECTING THE NEW WELLS TO THESE OLD ONES HERE.

NO ONE COMES HERE ANYMORE, EXCEPT FOR THE OCCASIONAL CARAVAN.

I RAISED FERDOS HERE.

I TOLD HIM OUR LEGENDS, SANG HIM POEMS, GAVE HIM ALL THE KNOWLEDGE OF OUR ANCIENT HOUSE, THE GUARDIANS OF THE WATER.

IF ANYONE HAD FOUND OUT, WE WOULD HAVE BOTH BEEN BEHEADED. FERDOS UNDERSTOOD...

...BUT STILL HE WAS THE HAPPIEST CHILD. AS HAPPY HERE AS A PRINCE. I COULD NEVER TAKE THAT AWAY FROM HIM. NO ONE CAN.

WHAT HAPPENED TO THE OTHER NEWBORNS?

SOMEWHERE OUT THERE, THEY SAY... SEVENTY-TWO BOYS ARE BURIED IN A PIT...

... WE MUST WALK LIKE CHILDREN AGAIN AND SEE THE MOON FOR THE FIRST TIME ...

... WHEN THERE IS NO WATER...

... THE ROOTS MUST DRINK OF DRYNESS AND LET THE FRUIT BE SWEETER STILL...

... FEAR NOT THE WAITING, BE LIKE BONES, DRY BONES...

... WHITE BONES, YOUR BONES...

... MY BONES.

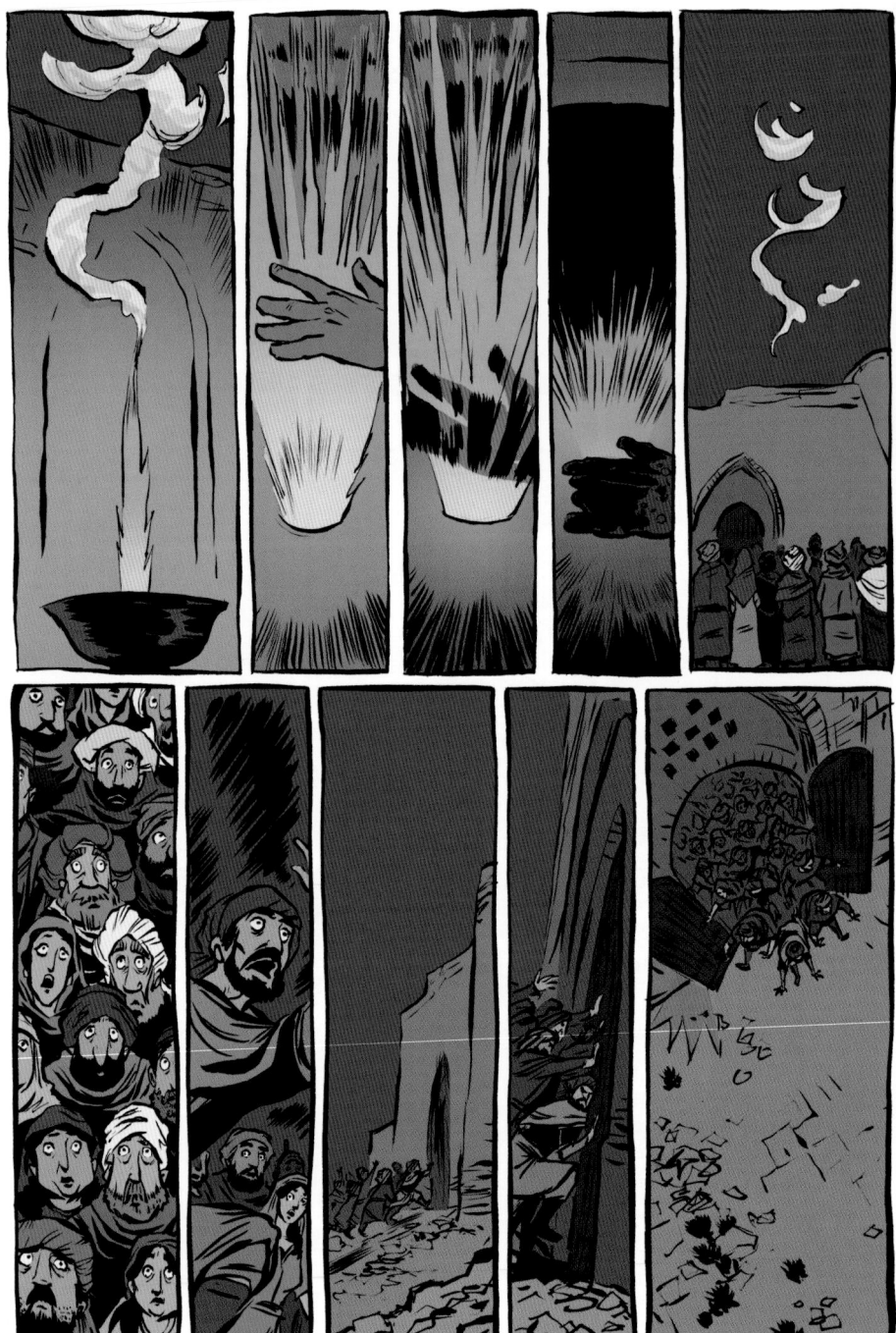

THERE'S NO ONE HERE.

THERE'S NO ONE THERE...

NO ONE BUT THE DEAD, THE DEAD...

PRINCESS, YOUR FACE IS AS THE MOON TONIGHT: AN ORB OF LIGHT IN OUR DARKNESS.

GENERAL AMIR, WHY ARE YOUR SOLDIERS ALL AROUND THE CITY AND THE PALACE?

THE PEOPLE ARE RESTLESS, FEARFUL. THE VEILED ONE OF MARV PROPHESIED THAT THE PALACE WILL BE BURNED DOWN. PERHAPS BY GUIV.

SO, PRINCESS, I THOUGHT PROTECTION MIGHT BE NECESSARY.

GENERAL, SUCH DECISIONS ARE TO BE MADE BY MY HUSBAND, LAYTH.

A PITY, THEN, THAT HE DOES NOT MAKE THEM.

TO QUELL RUMORS, I'M HAVING THE WORDS OF THAT VEILED FOOL TRANSCRIBED. WE MUST KNOW EXACTLY WHAT HE SAID.

HE SAID, "*FROM HENCE TWO HUNDRED AND FORTY-ONE YEARS.*" THAT PUTS US IN THE 481ST YEAR OF THE MOON.

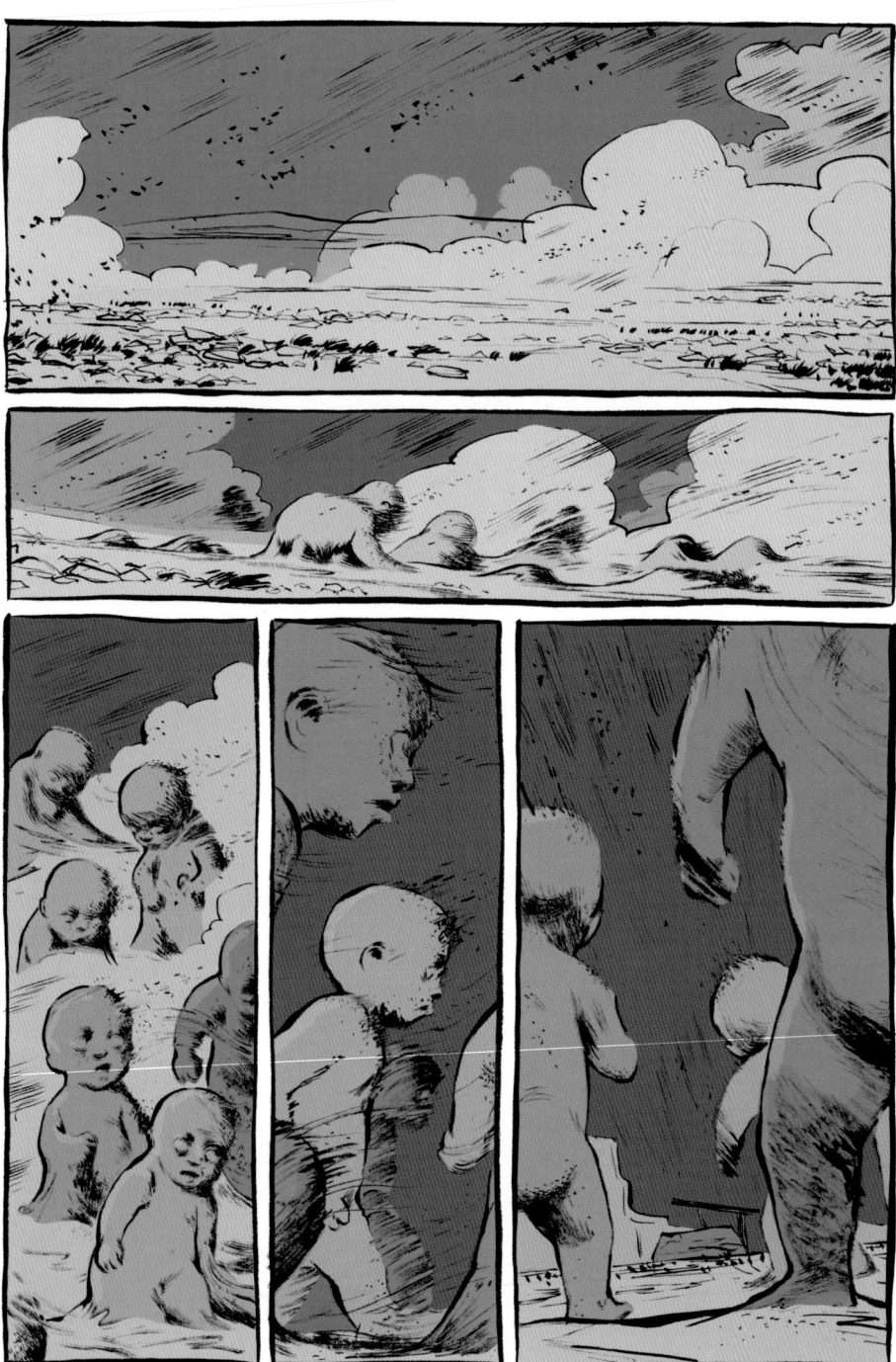

STOP! WHAT ARE YOU DOING?!

HE'S ONE OF US. WE'RE TAKING HIM BACK.

FATHER ?

STOP!

WATER, SHIRIN, WATER...

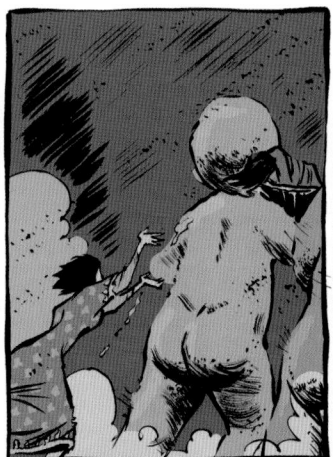

LEAVE OUR SONS ALONE!

WATER! WATER!

WATER! WATER!

IT'S NOTHING, LIGHT OF MY EYES... ONLY A NIGHTMARE.

NO... IT'S **REAL**... THE NIGHTMARE IS REAL... WE'RE PART OF IT.

MY LIGHT....

MY PEACOCK!

SHE'S NO PEACOCK, SHE'S A LIONESS. SHE'LL BE THE PRINCESS OF PERSIA, JUST LIKE YOU.

I WANTED TO BE THE PRINCE.

GLORIOUS MIDWIFE! TELL THE CITY, THE PEOPLE...

TELL THEM TO FORGET THE DONKEY-BRAINED PROPHECIES OF THE MADMAN IN THE MOUNTAINS. WE HAVE A NEW FUTURE TO CELEBRATE.

THE FUTURE IS NOT YET.

I CAN FEEL TIME MOVING AGAIN, CAN'T YOU? THE PAST HAS FALLEN AWAY... HOLD HER, YOU'LL KNOW WHAT I MEAN.

THE FUTURE IS HERE.

CLEAN THIS MESS UP AND BRING ME THE PRINCESS, UNHARMED AND WIDOWED.

PEACOCK ... PEACOCK ... WHERE HAVE YOU BEEN ...

BLAM
KLING

YOUR LIFE IS TOO WORTHLESS TO SWEAR BY.

IF ANYONE, ANYONE, IS DOWN ONE OF THESE WELLS, YOUR DEATH WILL BE WORTHLESS TOO.

YOU... SEARCH THE WELLS!

WHO'S DOWN THERE?

SPARE THE GUARDIAN. HE DID NOT SEE ME HIDE.

WAAAAAAAA...

RELEASE HER.

I OFFER YOU THE THRONE, LIGHT OF THE UNIVERSE. I SHALL STAND BESIDE YOU TILL THE END OF TIME.

NO! DON'T HARM HER!

LAYTH... MY LIGHT...

WHAT HAPPENED? WHY AM I DOWN HERE? IS THIS REAL? OR IS IT A NIGHTMARE?

THERE WERE PEOPLE OUTSIDE...

I'M FORGETTING...

I'M HUNGRY...

WHAT IN THE NAME...!

MY LION PELT.

WHAT LAW IS THIS?

WHAT BLOOD IS MY BLOOD? WHAT BLOOD?

THE BOOK IS INNOCENT. IT CANNOT SEE. IT CAN ONLY BE SEEN.

FERDOS, FORGIVE ME...

I HAD TO DO THIS, FOR YOU, FOR ME...

WHO'S THAT?

NO ONE FROM **OUR** ALLEY.

GRRROWWWLLL.

LEAVE HIM, HE'S JUST A CRAZY.

THAT'S NO GREAT FEAT, MY FRIENDS, WE'RE ALL BURNING SLOWLY HERE, IN THIS CITY GONE TO HELL.

NO PUBLIC GATHERINGS, CLEAR OUT, WE ARE IN A STATE OF EMERGENCY.

GET UP! CLEAR OUT!

'SCUSE ME, SIR, DO YOU KNOW WHERE ARSALAN'S DANCE SCHOOL IS?

IT'S NOT HERE, BOY.

WE HAVE OBLIGATIONS TO OUR LAND, TO OUR HISTORY...

... WE FIGHT WHAT THREATENS IT.

OVERCOMING EVIL IS NOBLE BUT HARD WORK WHEN OUR ENEMIES ARE AMONGST US.

AAAAAAH HHHHH!!

AAAAAAAHHHH!

BY ORDER OF THE COMMITTEE ON DANGERS PAST, PRESENT AND FUTURE...

WATCH WHAT YOU SAY! WATCH WHAT YOU DO!

WAIT! STOP!

WE CAN STOP THEM, DON'T YOU SEE?

CUT OFF HIS TONGUE TOO! CRAZY BEGGAR BOY!

BRING ME THAT PRISONER.

YOU MAY LEAVE. CARRY ON.

AAAAQAAAAHHHHHHHHHHH!

DAD?! YOU...!?
DO THIS...!?

WHERE HAVE YOU BEEN? EVERYONE'S BEEN LOOKING FOR YOU. YOU'RE A DISGRACE. YOU SHAME THE WHOLE FAMILY.

DAD! THEY'RE INNOCENT...

MY INNOCENT DAUGHTER, THERE IS NO MORE INNOCENCE. THESE ARE DANGEROUS PEOPLE WHO WANT TO END OUR GOOD LIFE. I WORK HARD SO THAT _YOU_ MAY LIVE PROSPEROUS AND SECURE.

AND LOOK AT YOU! LIKE A TURKISH BEGGAR BOY! WE'RE LUCKY NO ONE RECOGNIZED YOU! HOW'D I HAVE FACED THE GOVERNOR?

WASH UP AND LOOK RESPECTABLE! I'M TAKING YOU TO THE PALACE PARTY TOMORROW!

NO YOU'RE NOT!

ARSALAN!

I WENT TO THE WELL... I WAITED FOR YOU.

SIX OF OUR BROTHERS AND SISTERS WERE ARRESTED THAT NIGHT.

I... I'M SORRY.

COME.

LET THE FIRE RAGE, BY LOVE...

BURN LIKE A MOTH, BURN LIKE A MOTH.

BRING ON THE MADNESS, BRING DOWN THE HOUSE.

COME ROOM WITH US, GOOD FRIEND - IN THE HOUSE OF FIRE, IN THE HOUSE OF LOVE.

LAST WEEK WE LOST A HUNDRED AND THIRTY, ARRESTED.

WE'RE THE ONLY ONES LEFT.

WHERE'S YOUR PENDANT? YOU DON'T WEAR IT ANYMORE?

ARSALAN, I DIDN'T COME HERE TO SIT AROUND AND WAIT FOR HISTORY TO TEACH US ANOTHER LESSON.

THERE'S A PARTY TOMORROW AT THE PALACE. THE COMMITTEE WILL BE THERE.

WHAT CAN WE DO? WE'RE EIGHTEEN PEOPLE.

WE CAN BRING THE STARS DOWN TO EARTH.

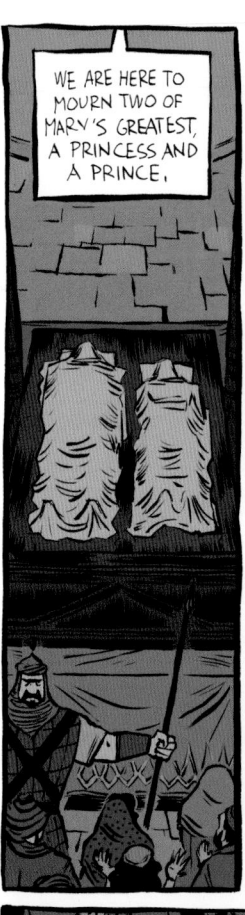

WE ARE HERE TO MOURN TWO OF MARV'S GREATEST, A PRINCESS AND A PRINCE.

IT IS ONLY WITH PROMISES AND FORGIVENESS THAT WE CAN BEGIN A FUTURE AND BIND OURSELVES TO IT.

THIS THEN IS MY PROMISE: I WILL BE AS JUST AS LAYTH, AS GOOD AS GUILAN, AND AS STRONG AS **AMIR**. THE UNKNOWN INCITERS WHO FELLED OUR LEADERS MUST BE FORGOTTEN, EVEN FORGIVEN...

FOR ONLY BY FORGIVING CAN WE INTERRUPT THE CYCLES OF VENGEANCE...

MURDERER! MURDERER!

WHOEVER THAT WAS, I FORGIVE HIM.

146

CRAK

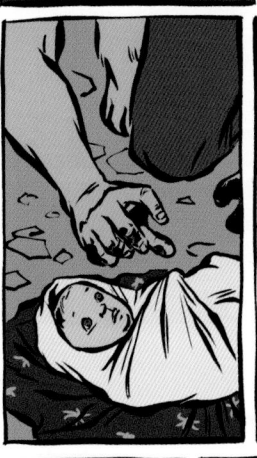

GUIN?
IN THE CITADEL?

HELLOOO?
OPEN UP!
PRINCE GUIN...

BAM
BAM
BAM

I BEG YOU—
OPEN UP!

SLAM

WHAT IS IT, GUARDIAN OF OUR WATERS?

THE PRINCESS IS DEAD, LAYTH TOO, SLAUGHTERED BY GENERAL AMIR.

WHAT DO YOU EXPECT ME TO DO ABOUT IT? AVENGE THEM?

WHY SHOULD THEIR DEATHS BE AVENGED ANY MORE THAN A THOUSAND OTHERS?

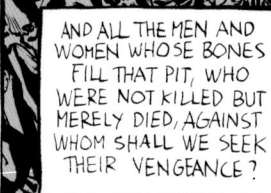

AND ALL THE MEN AND WOMEN WHOSE BONES FILL THAT PIT, WHO WERE NOT KILLED BUT MERELY DIED, AGAINST WHOM SHALL WE SEEK THEIR VENGEANCE?

SO IT'S TRUE WHAT THEY SAY IN THE BAZAAR. PRINCE GUIV IS GONE...

THE HOUSE OF SAMAN THE GREAT DIED THREE TIMES TODAY.

YAAAHRR!

YOU KNOW, OF COURSE, FOR WHAT I AM HERE.

UHH, TO GUIDE ME?

YES, GOOD, I WILL GO OVER THIS ONCE, NO MORE, YES? SADLY, YOU NOW HAVE HISTORY, AND HISTORY LOOKS LIKE THIS!

BLACK HAIR, SLENDER, 17 YEARS OLD, STIFF HIPS, EYES LIKE DATES, ONE GREEN, ONE YELLOW, SHE WAS HERE, NOW SHE IS NOT HERE: HISTORY.

OK, NOW AS FOR FUTURE: YOU WANT SIT HERE WITH MEMORIES? OR YOU WANT MAKE MORE NEW ONES, EVEN IF MAYBE BAD, MAYBE GOOD?

HEY?! WHERE YOU ARE?

68 NORTH, TO THE FIELDS...

I KNOW YOU'RE DOWN THERE.

WAIT!

HEY YOU!

KEEP YOUR PEACOCK ON A LEASH.

WHAT ARE YOU DOING? ARE YOU CRAZY COMING HERE? THERE'S A STATE OF EMERGENCY— SOLDIERS EVERY WHERE!

I NEED YOUR HELP.

WHAT HAVE YOU DONE? DID SOMETHING HAPPEN TO FERDOS? I KNEW YOU WERE BAD NEWS THE MOMENT I...

KRAK

YOU'RE UNDER ARREST.

BUT I'VE DONE NOTHING AT ALL.

DID YOU HEAR THAT? HE QUESTIONED HIS ARREST.

FORGIVE ME.

OUTTA THE WAY, PEACOCK BOY.

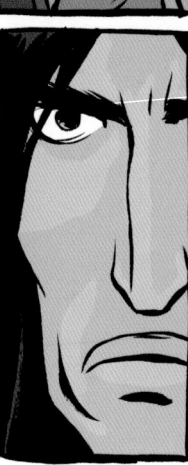

NOOO

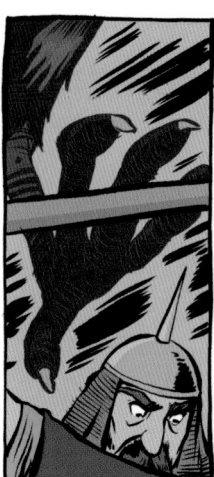

WHAT WAS THAT?

THEY'LL KILL ME, THEY'LL KILL YOU. OUR STORY HAS REACHED ITS END. OUR LINE OF GUARDIANS IS OVER...

... JUST POUR THE GRAVE DUST OVER MY HEAD RIGHT NOW.

IT'S ALL THIS CRAZY GIRL'S FAULT.

ENOUGH FATHER, LET'S GO!

COME, I KNOW A PLACE WHERE WE CAN HIDE.

THIS WAY.

WE WANTED TO TEACH HISTORY A LESSON, BUT THE TRUTH IS, HISTORY BENT US, WORE US DOWN...

...TAUGHT US TO GO ON OUR HANDS AND KNEES...

...WE HAVE LOST TOO MANY, IT'S TIME TO HANG UP OUR ARMS...

COME, FERDOS, WE HAVE NOTHING TO DO WITH THESE PEOPLE.

NO, WAIT.

...AND SIMPLY MOURN THE DEATH OF OUR SONS—ALL MURDERED SEVENTEEN YEARS AGO...

NOT ALL! ONE OF THEM SURVIVED!

WAAAAAAHHHHH...

YOU HEAR THAT?

A CRYING BABY.

HELLO, MY NAME IS FERDOS, PRINCE OF PARADISE.

SHHH, IT'S A SURPRISE PERFORMANCE.

SAY, ALI, WHAT IN THE WORLD IS THIS?

PLEASE, LET HIM GO. HE'S A FATHER, WE HAVE A DAUGHTER.

YES, I KNOW, MOTHER.

GROWNWL...

GUIV?

SO THE COWARD DESCENDS FROM THE HILLS LOOKING FOR HIS TWIN SISTER.

I SPARED HER LIFE, YOU KNOW, BUT SHE KILLED HERSELF.

SHE WAS ALWAYS STRONGER THAN YOU, AND WISER.

YOU'RE NOTHING WITHOUT HER!

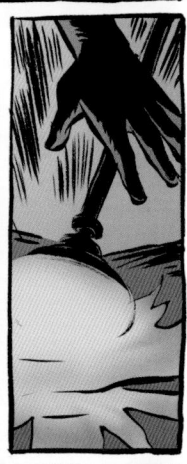

GUARDS!!

YOU TRAITORS!

YOU WON'T TAKE THIS PALACE...

YOU WON'T TAKE THIS THRONE!

I DIDN'T DO ANYTHING, MY DARLING, DON'T LISTEN TO THESE VAGABONDS!

SORRY, BABA, YOU WEIGH NO LIGHTER IN THE SCALES FOR BEING MY FATHER.

TELL THE GUARDS TO BACK OFF!

A MAN MUST BE BORN FROM A WOMB LIKE ANY OTHER WOMB.

FIRE IN THE PALACE, QUICK!

PSHHH

QUICK, PRINCE, MORE GUARDS ARE COMING!

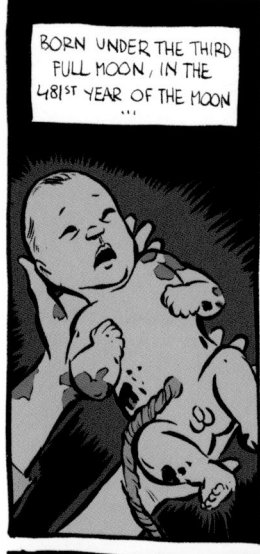

BORN UNDER THE THIRD FULL MOON, IN THE 481ST YEAR OF THE MOON...

...DEMANDS YOUR SURRENDER. IF YOU ACCEPT, YOU WILL LIVE UNDER HIS BENEVOLENT RULE.

IF NOT, WE WILL NOT SPARE ANY LIVES.

THE PEACOCK!

THE CITY IS UNDER SIEGE? WE DON'T STAND A CHANCE.

QUICK! FOLLOW ME!

THE FOOLS! THEY KNEW THEY WERE FINISHED.

WE'LL DEAL WITH THEM LATER.

SURRENDER IMMEDIATELY!

OPEN THE GATES.

WELCOME THE MONGOLS AS OUR SAVIORS.

KRAK

FOR HER, ONLY FOR HER,
MUST WE DIE.

BOOK, LIKE DOOR, IS
FOR TO BE CLOSED,
YAAAHR.

"But helpless Pieces of the Game He plays

Upon this Chequer-board of Nights and Days;

Hither and thither moves, and checks, and slays,

And one by one back in the Closet lays."

—Omar Khayyam, *Rubaiyat* (trans. Fitzgerald, 1879)

WHO IS THE PRINCE?

An Afterword by Jordan Mechner

Last year, while visiting UCLA's Powell Library, I saw a PlayStation 2 copy of *Prince of Persia: The Sands of Time* on display in a glass case alongside a 1903 edition of *The Arabian Nights*, a pack of Camel cigarettes, and a Las Vegas hotel ashtray with a picture of a harem girl. The title of the exhibition was "Seducing America: Selling the Middle Eastern Mystique."

It was an odd sensation finding my old familiar prince in such an unexpected place. I had lunch with the curator of the exhibit, an Israeli professor who collects twentieth century Orientalist pop-culture ephemera. I told him about the original *Prince of Persia* computer game, the one I'd programmed in the late 1980s. He was curious and asked where he might find a copy for his collection. You can download it for free, but what he really wanted was the box it came in.

BEGINNINGS

When I was twelve, I spent most of my free time drawing comics. I dreamed of a future with Bainbridge boards, T squares, and ink pen nibs.

Then the Apple II was invented.

A great thing about drawing comics is the intimacy of it. Hours vanish as you sit at your drawing board, absorbed in the characters and worlds you're creating. Comics were a perfect occupation for a kid inclined to daydreaming and solitude. So were computer games in the 1980s.

I found out quickly that I liked programming games and I liked animation—but what I loved was creating an imaginary universe that others could lose themselves in. The communion between game designer and player can be as personal as that between a novelist and reader. I wanted to create games that would not only challenge players but stir their emotions.

The Bainbridge boards went into the closet. I'd found a new obsession.

It was 1985. I'd just graduated from college. I was in my old bedroom in the town where I'd grown up: eating my parents' food, playing video games, and thinking about a game I wanted to make and that I hoped Broderbund Software would publish. I knew the kind of running, jumping, puzzle-solving acrobatic game play I wanted. What I needed was a story.

It was Broderbund's Gene Portwood (a former Disney animator) who spoke the magic words: "What about Ali Baba; Sinbad?"

On that muggy, rainy August afternoon, in a single burst of creative energy, I wrote a two-page story about a boy who sets out to win a princess's love by stealing an amulet from the dungeons of an evil sultan. I didn't stop to think, much less do research. Ideas and vivid images poured out faster than I could write them down. It was as if the characters had been there all along, lying dormant, stored in a dream, and now sprang to life—animating themselves in my head, running, jumping, and even speaking.

Rotoscoped animation frames for *Prince of Persia* (1989)

I must have met them somewhere before, but where? Maybe in some illustrated storybook I'd read as a child. Or on late-night TV, in those days when movies were fascinating, elusive things you couldn't own, couldn't freeze in time, could only glimpse as they flitted past, having no idea when or if the opportunity to see them might come again.

Where do stories come from? All I know is that when they do come, it's smart to get out of their way.

I moved to California and spent the next three years programming the game that would be *Prince of Persia*. The story line evolved, got tighter, streamlining and recombining elements. An evil sultan became a scheming vizier, a royal amulet was quietly dropped, a magic mirror was added.

One day I sat down at last and read *The Arabian Nights*. In those pages, I met my prince and princess, sultan and vizier, over and over in different guises. Shape-shifting, they peered out at me from behind different personas, like the broken fragments of a magic mirror.

Maybe the reason the land and characters of *The Arabian Nights* are so perfect for a video game is because they are themselves dreams. Peel away the layers of Western imaginings, the Hollywood harem girls and palm trees and, yes, video games that had fascinated my Israeli professor, and you find . . . more layers. Reading Husain Haddawy's excellent 1990 translation, I learned

that what I'd believed were the original unexpurgated *Nights*, brought to the West by Galland, Lane, and Burton in the eighteenth and nineteenth centuries, are actually a hodgepodge of translation, invention, and outright forgery that medieval Arabic scholars are still trying to unravel. Even Haddawy's version, probably the truest available, is based on copies of copies of tales that, by the time they were first written down in the ninth or tenth century, were already older than anyone could remember.

I hadn't created the prince. I'd had the luck to tap into a deep, centuries-old well of other people's dreams.

In 1992 a Russian writer named Victor Pelevin wrote a short story about a Soviet government functionary who plays *Prince of Persia* so much that the game starts to merge with his reality. Set in the late 1980s, at a time when the American computers needed to play games such as *Prince of Persia* were still in short supply, the story made the game famous in Russia.

"The little figure runs along the corridor. It is drawn with great affection, perhaps a little too sentimentally. If you press the <Up> key, it arches its back, and hangs in the air for a second, trying to catch hold of something above its head. If you press <Down> it squats and tries to pick something up from the ground under its feet. If you press <Right> it runs to the right, if you press <Left> it runs to the left. In fact you can use various keys to control it, but these four are the most important.

(…)

The final purpose is to reach the highest level, where the princess is waiting, but to do that you have to devote a lot of time to the game itself. In fact, to be successful, you have to forget that you're pressing keys and actually become the little figure— only then will it acquire the degree of agility required to fence, jump through the snapping body-scissors in the narrow stone corridors, leap over the stone shafts and run over the collapsing flagstones, each of which can only support the weight of a body for seconds—although the figure has no body, let alone any weight, and neither, if you think about it, do the tumbling slabs of stone, no matter how convincing the sound might be when they fall."

—Victor Pelevin, "Prince of Central Planning" (1992)

THE PRINCE ASSUMES A THOUSAND SHAPES

Given his slippery nature, it was inevitable that the prince would escape from my control. By 1992 *Prince of Persia* had become a worldwide best seller. Versions of the game were being sold on every computer and console platform I'd heard of and some I hadn't. Each new publisher and development team, in every country, put their own stamp on the graphics. The Super Nintendo prince didn't look quite like the Sega Genesis prince or the Sharp X68000 prince, the prince on the front of the box didn't look like the prince in the screen shots on the back, and some of them made me cringe.

I had no one to blame but myself. I'd chosen to present my story stripped down to its bare essentials, with characters that conveyed their personalities through gesture and action, not words. This left plenty of space for others to fill the void with their own imaginings.

Who is the prince? Does he have a name? How old is he? Is he a prince to start with, or does he become one by

Prince of Persia in Japan: Super FamiCom *Prince of Persia* box (1992)

marrying the princess? What land is he from, who are his parents, what is the sultan a sultan of, and what century is it anyway?

"Long ago in a certain city there lived a king . . ." *The Arabian Nights* tales rarely got more specific than that about time and place, and neither did 1980s video games. Baghdad or Samarkand, the ninth century or the twelfth—what did it matter so long as there was a scheming vizier, a beautiful princess, and a palace on a moonlit night? On the 280 x 192 screen of the Apple II, where the characters' faces were four pixels square, such details hardly seemed to matter.

Amiga *Prince of Persia* box (1990)

But as the 1980s became the 1990s, as video-game technology improved, and teams of artists and engineers I would never meet began translating *Prince of Persia* to platforms with more memory and higher-resolution graphics, those questions I'd left unanswered started to chafe.

In 1993 Broderbund published the prince's second adventure, *The Shadow and the Flame*. Hoping to preempt the proliferation of princes and inconsistent backstories that my first game had spawned, I'd written up what I intended to be a definitive "bible" establishing the prince's past once and for all—as George Lucas had done for *Star Wars*, planting the seeds that would flower in future episodes.

Concept art for *Sands of Time* (2003). Copyright © Ubisoft Entertainment. All rights reserved.

Even while I was writing it, I'd had a vague sense that it didn't feel quite right. In hindsight, I think my real problem was that in trying to force *Prince of Persia* into the Western, Nordic epic-trilogy-struggle-between-good-and-evil format that had worked for Lucas—and Tolkien and Wagner before him—I'd failed to take into account the prince's origins as an *Arabian Nights* character. Those were tales of wisps and dreams, whose nature was to spin and embroider themselves out of nothing, only to vanish again in the shimmering mist. In Wagner, everything is destiny. In the *Nights*, anything can happen.

As it turned out, I never got the chance to complete my epic trilogy. The big video-game sensation of 1993 was *Doom*, the first 3-D shooter. The public no longer wanted 2-D platformers; plans for a third *Prince of Persia* game were quietly shelved. Six years later, Broderbund tried to catch up by releasing *Prince of Persia 3D*, but the project was plagued by difficulties, and landed not with a bang but a whimper.

It seemed that the prince's adventures had run their course. And, I told myself, maybe that wasn't entirely a bad thing. He'd traveled so far from his origins, I hardly recognized him anymore.

In 2003, the prince got that rarest of things: a second chance.

When I joined Ubisoft Montreal as writer and game designer of the title we hoped would revive the all-but-dead *Prince of Persia* franchise, the team faced a daunting challenge. The best-remembered title in the series, the first one, was almost fourteen years old. In video-game years, that's an eternity.

Fittingly, the tale we chose to tell was about second chances. *Prince of Persia: The Sands of Time* is the story of a young warrior who is tricked by the villain into making a terrible mistake that threatens to destroy

Character model for *Sands of Time* (2003). Copyright

not only his kingdom, but the fabric of reality itself. Only through heroic effort, helped by a princess he loves but is never quite sure whether to trust, can he set things right.

From the original game we took an hourglass; the basic triangle of prince, princess, and vizier; and a certain style of game play. The rest was new. The tremendous advance in graphics and sound technology meant that a team of talented artists could realize the prince's world with greater beauty and detail than ever before.

A decade and a half after he'd first run and jumped across an Apple II screen, the pixelly prince found his footing: ninth-century Persia—a time of warfare and intrigue, perfect for a tale of romance and adventure.

Doing research for *Sands of Time*, I picked up the *Shahnameh*, the Persian Book of Kings, set in verse a thousand years ago by the great poet Ferdosi. Reading the complete work for the first time, in an edition beautifully illustrated with sixteenth-century Persian miniatures, was a revelation to me.

The *Shahnameh* represents a different tradition from *The Arabian Nights*. Its epic tales of kings and heroes are to the East what Norse mythology is to northern Europe. A Persian prince like the one in *Sands of Time* would have grown up steeped in the oral tradition of the *Shahnameh*; he would have spoken about the strength of Rustam the way a 20-year-old soldier today might casually refer to Superman or the Hulk. (And, in *Sands of Time*, he does.) But as much as the prince aspires to resemble the noble warriors of the *Shahnameh*, doomed to fulfill their heroic destinies, he can't quite shed the basically happy-go-lucky nature of an *Arabian Nights* prince, stumbling from one adventure into the next. It's his inability to resolve this conflict that gives him his particular charm.

⤟⤞

Ubisoft followed up *Sands of Time* with two sequels, *Warrior Within* and *The Two Thrones*, which gave the prince a more ruthless, violent edge. They're hard at work now in Montreal crafting his next adventure, which promises

Concept art for *The Two Thrones* (2005).

to feel closer in spirit to the romantic fantasy of *Sands of Time* and of the original game.

Jerry Bruckheimer and Walt Disney Pictures are making a *Prince of Persia* movie. I wrote the screenplay, but I won't be surprised if in his journey to the screen, the prince once again transforms into a somewhat different shape than I'd initially envisioned. This prince is a survivor. In the past two decades, he's shown himself more adaptable and resilient than I ever expected.

Will the actor who plays the prince in the movie become the real, definitive Prince of Persia? Will he supplant the prince in the video games? Can so many princes coexist peacefully?

Or are they all somehow the same person?

GAMES TO COMICS

In 2004 I got an e-mail from Mark Siegel, the editor of a new publishing imprint called First Second Books. He told me that *Prince of Persia* had had a special place in his heart since the early 1990s, when he'd first played it on a black-and-white Macintosh Classic. Would I be interested in developing it as a graphic novel?

He didn't know he was offering to fulfill one of my childhood dreams.

As Mark and I got to know each other, we found out that we had a lot in common—including a passion for the French hardcover graphic novels called *bandes dessinées*. I'd fallen in love with the work of Hugo Pratt, Enki Bilal, and François Schuiten in my twenties, when I spent a year in France. Their books had been a huge influence on my video-game writing, especially *The Last Express* and *Sands of Time*. When Mark told me that one of his missions for First Second is to foster European-quality graphic novels in the United States, I got even more excited.

And when artists LeUyen Pham and Alex Puvilland came on board, with their rich backgrounds in children's illustration and Dreamworks feature animation, we were more certain than ever that a graphic novel about the prince's adventures could be something special.

The question was, which prince?

The plucky Aladdin-like street urchin of the first game? The orphan-with-a-mythic-destiny of *The Shadow and the Flame*? The guilt-ridden young warrior of *Sands of Time*? The battle-hardened fugitive he became in *Warrior Within* and *The Two Thrones*? Or the prince of the *Sands of Time* movie—or

rather of the screenplay, which will have been rewritten many times over by the time cameras roll?

Which one is the true Prince of Persia? All of them. And none of them.

Our search for a writer who could encompass this paradox led us to the mysterious and reclusive A. B. Sina.

When A. B. asked us what we expected him to write, we said we weren't sure, exactly, but the connection to the video games should be deep below the surface, not evident at first glance. We didn't want an adaptation of any of the games or of the movie, but a new story that would tap into the deep wellspring of Persian myth, legend, and history from whence the prince had arisen.

A. B. thought about it for a bit, then remarked that in the tales of the East—from *The Arabian Nights* to Sufi stories—the characters' conflicts and relationships tend to be with the structure of reality itself, the structure of consciousness, rather than with individual psychological issues as we tend to focus on in the West. He pointed out that the struggle against destiny is the most universal of all struggles, that it fuels the American myths and the American dream, as well as Eastern ones.

We were off and running.

❦

Playing video games is all about timing, so it's not too surprising that in every *Prince of Persia* story so far, time itself has been a central motif.

What is interesting is that with each iteration, the time frame seems to expand. The first game was confined to the hour it took for the sands in Jaffar's hourglass to run out. *Sands of Time* took place over several days, with the menace embodied by a different kind of hourglass. The *Sands of Time* movie screenplay paints a broader canvas and takes place over weeks. And the graphic novel spans centuries—specifically, two parallel stories unfolding four centuries apart.

A. B. has woven a delightfully subversive tale offering us not just one, but many Persian princes. All in their different ways fighting wild beasts and magical creatures, falling in love with princesses, and falling afoul of scheming viziers, as my prince had done for at least a thousand years before he ran and jumped through a late-summer rainstorm onto the Apple II computer screen.

One of the possible princes in A. B. Sina's story wonders if he is prophesying the future, or if the future is remembering him.

A sentiment the original Prince of Persia, wherever he is, must surely sympathize with.

Los Angeles
October 2007

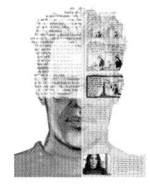

THE AMAZING REMARKABLE MONSIEUR LEOTARD

By Eddie Campbell & Dan Best

An adventure following the turn-of-the-century life of the amazing and remarkable Monsieur Leotard, Acrobat and Circus Manager, both before and after his tragic death by misadventure.

SLOW STORM

By Danica Novgorodoff

Tornado season in Kentucky brings together an illegal immigrant and a firefighter struggling with her job and family in this powerful American drama about homesickness, horses, storms, and saints.

THE BLACK DIAMOND DETECTIVE AGENCY

By Eddie Campbell

"A turn-of-the-century pulp thriller." – *Kirkus*

THE LOST COLONY
Book 1: The Snodgrass Conspiracy

By Grady Klein

"[A] witty, sophisticated, candy-colored adventure." – *Booklist*

THE LOST COLONY
Book 2: The Red Menace

By Grady Klein

"Insightful satire . . . willingness to suspend PC tsk-tsking comes in handy [for] enjoying . . . Klein's skewering re-enactment of the bad old days." – *Booklist*

 **THE PROFESSOR'S DAUGHTER**

By Emmanuel Guibert & Joann Sfar

"No glorified comic book, this graphic novel aspires to fine art."
★ – *Kirkus*, STARRED REVIEW
★ *BCCB*, STARRED REVIEW

DRAWING WORDS & WRITING PICTURES

By Jessica Abel & Matt Madden

"A gold mine of essential information for every aspiring comics artist. Highly recommended."
– Scott McCloud, author of *Understanding Comics*

LIFE SUCKS

By Jessica Abel, Gabe Soria, and Warren Pleece

Life sucks for Dave Marshall – he hates his job, the girl he's in love with doesn't know he exists, and to top it all off, his boss just turned him into a vampire.

★ LAIKA

By Nick Abadzis

"A luminous masterpiece filled with pathos and poignancy."
★ – *Kirkus*,
STARRED REVIEW
Publishers Weekly,
STARRED REVIEW

GARAGE BAND

By Gipi

" . . . real teens struggling to find their paths in life, sorting out what really matters to them." – *VOYA*

JOURNEY INTO MOHAWK COUNTRY

By George O'Connor

"The book's quality ensures its place in studies of pre-Revolutionary America." – *Kirkus*

A.L.I.E.E.E.N.

By Lewis Trondheim

"Readers will be delighted by this wordless tale with endearing, yet rascally alien characters." – *Kirkus*

 Winner of the INTERNATIONAL HORROR GUILD'S AWARD for 'Best Illustrated Narrative.'

★ DEOGRATIAS
A Tale of Rwanda

By J.P. Stassen

"The importance of the story and the heartbreaking beauty of its presentation make it an essential purchase."
★ – *Kirkus*, STARRED REVIEW

★ KAMPUNG BOY

By Lat

"This companionable chronicle achieves that rare thing in an international title: making readers feel like they're hanging out with a friend halfway around the world."
★ – *BCCB*, STARRED REVIEW
★ *Booklist*, STARRED REVIEW
★ *School Library Journal*, STARRED REVIEW

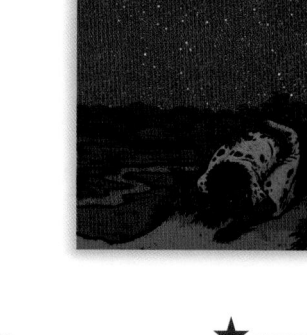

★ MISSOURI BOY

By Leland Myrick

"The tenderness and intimacy of the spare words and pictures . . . set the book apart."
★ – *Booklist*,
STARRED REVIEW

Especially for YOUNG READERS

LITTLE VAMPIRE
By Joann Sfar

Three stories about an unusual friendship, including the *New York Times* bestseller 'Little Vampire Goes to School,' by the inimitable Joann Sfar.

★ ROBOT DREAMS
By Sara Varon

"Exhibit A to prove that graphic novels can pack an emotional punch equal to some of the best youth fiction."
★ – *Booklist*, STARRED REVIEW
★ *Publishers Weekly*, STARRED REVIEW
★ *School Library Journal*, STARRED REVIEW

★ SARDINE IN OUTER SPACE
By Emmanuel Guibert & Joann Sfar

"Resistance is futile." ★ – *Kirkus*, STARRED REVIEW

"With the usual sly humor and gleefully childlike sense of the absurd, Guibert and Sfar offer bizarre, memorable characters and a delightfully surreal story." – *Booklist*

TINY TYRANT
By Lewis Trondheim & Fabrice Parme

"A real treat for classic-cartoon fans of many ages."
– *Booklist*

KAPUT & ZÖSKY
By Lewis Trondheim & Eric Cartier

Universal obliterators Kaput and Zösky are at the top of their game – so why does their world conquering fail so dismally?

AND MORE GEMS AT **www.firstsecondbooks.com**

Special thanks to Tanya McKinnon, Florence Baccard, Hayden Walling,
Julie Henson, Sally Wheeler, Ryan Cole, Terry Sycamore,
Kat Kopit, Gina Gagliano, and Siena Siegel

:01

First Second

New York & London

Published by First Second
First Second is an imprint of Roaring Brook Press,
a division of Holtzbrinck Publishing Holdings Limited Partnership
175 Fifth Avenue, New York, NY 10010

Distributed in Canada by H. B. Fenn and Company Ltd.
Distributed in the United Kingdom by Macmillan Children's Books, a division of Pan Macmillan.

Book design by Mark Siegel and Danica Novgorodoff

Library of Congress Cataloging-in-Publication Data

Sina, A. B.
Jordan Mechner's Prince of Persia / by AB Sina ; art by LeUyen Pham with Alex Puvilland.
p. cm.
ISBN: 978-1-59643-207-9
1. Graphic novels. I. Pham, LeUyen. II. Puvilland, Alex. III. Mechner, Jordan. IV. Title. V. Title:
Prince of Persia.
PN6727.S527J67 2008
741.5'973--dc22
2007015504

ISBN: 978-1-59643-602-2

First Second books are available for special promotions and premiums.
For details, contact: Director of Special Markets, Holtzbrinck Publishers.

First Edition September 2008
Printed in December 2009 in China by C&C Joint Printing Co., Shenzhen, Guangdong Province
1 3 5 7 9 10 8 6 4 2